Praise for *Sonny Kenner's Red Guitar*:

This book is like being at a wonderful party where you know
only a few of the people but get caught up in the conversation,
in the music, in whatever is happening, and before you know it
morning is almost here and you're still here, too, in the energetic
intimacy of the continuous present. Rich with characters who
show up a memorable once, or reappear like that couple you met
last year at the same bar—there they are, still together!—these
poems arrive. Rabas writes narrative as if it's part of a jazz song,
a sudden fillip of melody, while somewhere off in the margin the
drums hold things together. You can't help joining in, nodding,
turning each page.
                                        —Elizabeth Dodd, *Horizon's Lens*

Not only do these poems flourish with sensuality, they sing with
what makes poetry most important: compassion. Rabas brings
kindness to reality, splendor to simple moments, and music to
life.
                                        —Matthew Porubsky, *Ruled by Pluto*

Rabas knows the American Midwestern sub-suburban/small
town/back roads experience down to the very fiber of that rough
fabric (damn-near to the sub-atomic level). He knows the jazz
afflicted country kid's big dreams of big cities, bright lights and
decent paying gigs and that those dreams usually lead us to plac-
es we never imagined. He knows what it is to be on the business
end of Love's wind-up haymaker to the heart and what it means
to really ache and moan late at night for those lost moments that
always seem to come back to us as "could have/should have/too
little, too late, too bad." Most importantly, Rabas knows the an-
cient, tribal, hoo-doo secrets of distilling all of these things into
the bracing after-dinner liqueur of PO-try. He's also a hell of a
nice guy. He even let me crash at his place once. Still gives me a
strange look out of the corner of his eye, to this day.
                                        —Jason Ryberg, *Down, Down and Away*

ALSO BY KEVIN RABAS:

POETRY
Bird's Horn & Other Poems
Lisa's Flying Electric Piano

FICTION
Spider Face: stories

Sonny Kenner's Red Guitar

POEMS
by Kevin Rabas

Coal City Review 31   May 2013

Brian Daldorph, Editor
University of Kansas
English Department
Lawrence
KS 66045

briandal@ku.edu

Thanks to Pam LeRow, CLAS Digital Media Services,
University of Kansas

Printed by Lightning Source

Thanks to the Neptune Foundation

ISBN 13: 978-0-9795844-6-6
ISBN 10: 0-9795844-6-9

Cover artwork: "Love Over Fear" by Jennifer Rivera
Cover design: Tamar Jaffe Reyes
tamarelisejaffe@gmail.com
Author photo by: Stephan Anderson-Story

To contact the author:
Kevin Rabas
PO Box 274
Emporia, KS 66801
krabas3@yahoo.com or krabas@emporia.edu
kevinrabas.com

2nd printing, March 2014

Acknowledgements:

The author gratefully acknowledges the editors of the following publications, in which versions of the following poems first appeared:

"A Star," *Cybersoleil Journal*
"At 21," *Thunderclap*
"Background Jazz," *The Little Balkans Review*
"Birds Here," *seveneightfive*
"Dee," *Touch Poetry*
"Fables of Faubus," *Xavier Review*
"From the Suburbs," *Muddy River Poetry Review*
"forget every bird," *Connecticut Review*
"*for* the estranged," *Mikrokosmos*
"Kissing Bea," "We Read," *Begin Again: 150 Kansas Poems*
"Last Night at The Blue Room," *The Whirlybird Anthology of Kansas City Writers*
"Like One of Joe's Songs," "Samantha's Twin Toddler Sons," *Thorny Locust*
"Liz Catches Stars," *Seltzer*
"Pictographs Somewhere in the Pahrocs," *Nimrod*
"Pheasant Hunting Sketch," *Plains Song Review*
"Set in Some Parts of Kansas," *Parcel*
"Skate Party," *Rethink Topeka*
"Sonny Kenner," *The Café Review*
"Steamboat Erupts," "White Tea," *Sheridan Edwards Review*
"When the Writers Gather and Drive," *Blue Island Review*
"Wild Horses & Road," "Gwen," *Midwestern Gothic*
"Your Almost Blunted Purpose," *The Poetry Bus*

Winner of the Nelson Poetry Book Award

Words of Thanks:

I am blessed to have a family that appreciates and encourages my writing, including Lisa, Eliot, Joyce, Gary, and Alicia. Since I was very young, my mother set me on this path—to write—through her encouragement and through her example as a newspaper writer, reporter, and editor. Also, I think my mother has read almost every book at the Shawnee library, setting the example that to write one must read deeply and widely. I am indebted to her example—and her guidance. Thank you, Mom. Thanks also go to my writer and artist friends, who read this manuscript (or early parts of it) and gave advice, notes, and encouragement, including Dennis Etzel Jr., Sarah Smarsh, Matthew Porubsky, Joseph DeLuca, Laura Cossey, Val Bontrager, Joyce Rabas, Selah Saterstrom, Denise Low, Dan Jaffe, Elizabeth Dodd, Tyler Sheldon, Alex Arceneaux, Jason Ryberg, Marina Jaffe, Ruth Moritz, Richard Warner, Amy Sage Webb, Bill Sheldon, William Clamurro, and Lisa Moritz. Thanks also go to the cover design work of Tamar Jaffe Reyes. Many thanks also go to Jennifer Rivera, who offered a painting especially for this book cover. Many thanks also go to my editor and publisher Brian Daldorph.

Thanks also to Pam LeRow for final text and cover layout and design—and to Joyce Rabas for final text copyediting. Thanks also go to Alicia (Rabas) Styles and Sam Styles for advice on how to portray the wilderness with accuracy. Thanks also go to jazz and blues historian Chuck Haddix for his bio of Sonny Kenner, which captures Kenner's spirit and reach. And thanks to Sonny Kenner, the musician, whose playing inspired this book's title.

for Joyce Rabas

for the mosquito, too,
the night is long—
long and lonely.
                                  —Issa

Contents:

IV. travel & place

Introduction

I'm thankful to be introducing another terrific collection
by my friend Kevin Rabas. I've watched these poems develop,
grow, and search for readers. Kevin's poems are doors into the
place where poetry helps us when we need it the most. Even the
first poem is an invitation, as much as it is an invocation, for all
of the estranged. The music of this poem doesn't let go of you,
just like jazz musicians and poets all know, just as Kevin says:

> full of my loneliness and nights
> spent alone in the dark, new-moon nights,
> coal-colored nights, nights where the owl call
> is for you; I hear you; I see you; I will be
> with you, when you open to this page; yours
> will never be nights alone; my voice is here
> with you, across time, across space; and when
> you sing, I am here—on rhythm guitar, on bass,
> on drums, on harpsichord and violin.

Kevin's poetry is the enactment of connecting, of connec-
tions with other people. In the same way he connects to people
through his music, these beats, these figures of language, these
figures of love, still have my attention throughout the various
forms this book has taken.

Of course, Jazz plays a big part in Kevin's life and poems.
What I call "musician portraits" are in his work, including in this
collection.

> We're playing on the street, in the square,
>   in Barcelona, a little jazz
> group with a lot of hand
>   drummers—and I'm playing
> on trash: milk carton, box,
>   Snapple bottle. ("Tip Bucket")

The improvisation Kevin takes on riffs on a beat to create a
poem. These portraits are like elegies, too, for musicians gone
or passed away: "I say, 'It sounds like it has the feel / of one of
Joe's tunes,' and she says / she was thinking of him when she
wrote it" ("Like One of Joe's Songs"). The history of Jazz is
parallel with stories of gigs and late nights. Kevin lets us in on

these amazing performers, including singers that can "turn / a flat penny on its side" ("Megumi").

Along with the heart for Jazz, there is a lot of heart in the stories derived from Kevin's past, through the narratives of ebb and flow, desire and loss, and of portraits and self-reflections. His sharing of the personal pays off in his aesthetics:

> Samantha's husband had gone crazy and left her
> for a VJ he found on the web.
> I too had once gone crazy,
> but I swore I would not go crazy again.

These stories—along with the internal dialogue—hit swiftly. There is just enough of event to allow these poems to occupy the reader's space of personal decision, loss, regret, and survival.

Sometimes this survival itself occupies the space, too, as place mirrors emotional atmosphere: "Lisa calls from her motel. She has locked / herself out. She's in the cold, keyless, some-where / in lonesome Boulder" ("Lisa Calls from Boulder Colorado"). The poet's imagination and compassion embodies the poem, as we are sympathetic for the writer:

> but even in summer
> it can be cold, August,
> and my lover is locked out, calling, asking what to do
> about cold quiet Colorado.

Kevin has a skill in balancing these narratives, both inner and outer places, which makes reading a pleasure.

Ultimately, I cherish this collection as the poems enact the power to help. Poetry helps us in that way William Carlos Williams defines and laments: "men [and women] die miserably every day for lack of what is found there." Kevin's voice, style, and message is something to carry:

> Your voice is the one I tune to
> when the streets grow cold
> and empty—and when
> the traffic becomes too much. ("Forget Every Bird")

Thank you, Kevin, for sharing your poetic voice when streets cannot help.

Dennis Etzel Jr.
September 2012

I.
for the estranged

For the estranged; the ones
the door shuts to with a wood
and metal click; to the lonely;
the ones who would be
lovers, but their loves walked off
with the pretty, with the slick, the rich;
to the ones with five string guitars who
play and save for that snapped
sixth string; for the drummers
with beat up drums
who keep their heads tuned
the best they can and play soft and wait
and wait for that crescendo and fill it
with grain, with water, with blue fire—
with a crowd of new hands: hands
and wheat, hands and wheat, hands and wheat;
to the ones you ignore, but never
ignore you; this poem of love
is for the ones, the estranged; this poem
full of my loneliness and nights
spent alone in the dark, new-moon nights,
coal-colored nights, nights where the owl call
is for you; I hear you; I see you; I will be
with you, when you open to this page; yours
will never be nights alone; my voice is here
with you, across time, across space; and when
you sing, I am here—on rhythm guitar, on bass,
on drums, on harpsichord and violin.

When the Writers Gather and Drive
AWP Austin, for Amy Sage Webb

Amy, a foodie, says she knows about this great place outside
of Austin, and we gather around my car in the Hilton parking
garage, which is lit like a cave. We can't get the child's seat out,
and so Amy volunteers to sit in it. I have on my first pair of roper
cowboy boots since I was 12, and I floor it, unintentionally, and
we barrel out of the Hilton parking garage and into the purple
Texas night, four writers looking for fine food on the outskirts of
town, down and around lots of curves and rises and falls in the
road, Amy, perched like a baby bird, in my toddler's child seat.
Like a scene from *Wonder Boys*, movie of writers and their cars;
Grady Trip's trunk holds a dead dog, a tuba, and a set of suitcases
perfectly, just like in the ad. Although I'm driving, Amy is in the
lead, saying, "Go left here. Now straight through the next two
lights. Now right." Bart is in the backseat with Amy, and he says,
"There are almost no families with siblings who are writers. The
Bronte Sisters, the Brothers Grimm, they are the exceptions.
We're alone in our families." "But we're all brothers and sisters
here," someone says, and Jeffrey tilts his ballcap back, and I step
a little harder on the pedal, and we scale a series of small curves.
Like a rollercoaster climbing, we make our way up the mountain
and to the restaurant that looks like a cabin from the outside.
Inside, it's finer than the Ritz, and we take shots in the entrance,
using my disposable camera, pulled from a pocket and snapped
into light. This is the life you never hear of, the once a year
gathering of the birds, of the tribe. There are a bunch of us, say
8000. But we live all over the country, and there seem to be no
two in one town, people who choose paper over television, legal
pad and quick pen script over that email or Facebook you're
just dying to write, people who watch and write down what the
neighbors do and do not do, who record the town, in secret, for
about 35K a year, and sink into ecstasy when a small press picks
up what they have written and prints it, and it stays in print, in a
few libraries and in the homes of friends, decades after the writer
passes, a record, a sketch of that time, traced and retraced until it
almost takes on paint, the way revision works. Someone spent a

lifetime writing and rewriting a moment, a scene depicting your life, and that someone is speeding down curves, in a loaded car, full of wine and fine food, the best meal they may ever have had, and that is the way of it, once a year, when the writers gather, Webb in the coxswain spot, giving directions, as the car sways and rumbles, writes its way into the oncoming night.

Kissing Bea on the Prairie

Bea tells me to turn off the road
at a silo in a part of Leoti
she does not know. The prairie grasses
around us move as an ear on a cat would
to listen, the way stalks on sunflowers tilt
to put sun in their seeds and petals.
It is dark—the shade of well water,
and the stars are not ours, but we see them
up there, like sequins on a black dress.
Bea takes off her underwear,
and it falls into the heather. I take off
her shirt, and my hands hold her
as if it is my first time, my fingers
like rain that runs over the body.
Her shirt and bra go
to my car hood, and her knee
is at my belt loop, and the car lights come
down that long dirt road and speed by.
Then, the dark Camaro backs up,
and we are in our car, too, being chased
into town. All I have known
are the suburbs with their street signs
and traffic lights, and their waxed police cruisers
on nearly every corner, and then
there is Bea, a prairie girl; I've known her only five months,
and the land that brought her up: the heather
in autumn, the valleys that hold a little water,
and the sparse shelter belts that call in the birds.
We beat the other car into town, and it turns,
and vanishes, and we wonder if that was their land—
if they chased us for violence or sport. I rest
my hand on Bea's thigh, and we quit thinking, quit
speaking, and kiss.

Sonny Kenner has his red guitar
in hand, and moves through the melody as if what he wants
is for everyone now to give and get that long kiss
in this room on this night in this club, in the Levee,
where I am dancing with Adrienne for the first time,
and her hips have got me dancing better than I have ever
danced before, and I want to just shimmy on up to her and take her
by the waist and lead her on out into this street lamp night
and onto a quilted patch blanket in this city grass,
beneath these tall alders—and let our howls
be to a new moon, and to the city fountains,
and to the plaza holiday lights that might flicker and blink on
in the middle of summer just for us, our lust flipping that switch,
that strand of wire in the bulb heating and glowing,
for one eyebat wink.

We Read

At the Olpe Chicken House behind glass there's a copy
of Ken Ohm's new book *Ducks Across the Moon*.
An old woman and her husband cane their way
to the counter, pay with cash, the bills
old and crumbled and green, and ask about the book.
The kid behind the counter, who looks like the town
quarterback, says, "I didn't write it," annoyed.
"Heck, I don't know." And the old couple walk on,
go home, mention books they do know and love,
and they read under white light, and slump in peace, sleep
on their La-Z-Boys, the tv snow, the books
held in their laps, their reading lamps still on.

How to Begin

Calvin gave himself half an hour
  to write like it was the end,
his last 30 minutes up top, above—
  on dirt, in sun, alive with breath and penscratch.

But he only wrote two anecdotes
and part of a letter and a comment/critique
to a new student. The letter
was to his sister.

This is how it is. We do
what we always do, even
in the end. So we must train
ourselves to do last things, true
things, bright things with each breath.
Call your mother and father.
Write that last pale blue check.

Set in Some Parts of Kansas

I.

At the road sign for the Flying J, I pull over, and Julie and I
run circles in the newly cut milo, the short stalks tan with red
speckles, as when a winged rooster pheasant falls and runs
through and leaves a blood spot trail. We're two college kids
from the suburbs in a field, catching a brief feel of country.

II.

Charlie Parker's Toronto plastic saxophone, especially made,
played once, is propped behind glass at the American Jazz
Museum. Parker was from KCK, a farm. *A Love Supreme* opens
with rooster sounds on sax, the sun rising. In The Blue Room
Gerald Dunn is on sax, his eyes tight shut, his sax bright in stage
light, his fingers bringing out the notes; his chest rising, he brings
in more breath—his own sound, but also Parker in the room, like
cigarette smoke snake trails, like ice cubes kissing in gin and
tonic, like the warmth of a low, full note warming your entire
chest.

III.

Green and tall with whiskers in the air, the hard red winter wheat
is more than up—and my grandmother is in the field with her
two remaining sons, both in their 30s; they take hold of her and
hug her in Carhartts in the last golden rays of Kansas light in a
summer that for this one evening has turned purple and cool.

IV.

We cruise Johnson Drive in Mission in my '67 Mustang
fastback, 289, white with red interior, with vents like fish gills,
letting the autumn breeze in. Gene has his ballcap turned back,
and Erica has her hand in the wind, her long blond hair a stream
of sunlight. A cop car pulls up behind and follows us for eighteen
blocks, then turns, and we put our hands out again, and we feel
like we are stealing something.

Last Night at The Blue Room

On that night, everyone
Calvin ever loved (or knew)
showed up at The Blue Room,
almost all of them
with someone else.

Pale Elizabeth E. came with a black flautist,
and she had an arm length cast
from her elbow to her left wrist.
A redhead, she wore pink. He sat in.

Hallie came with her camera and took shots
of the band, her hair dyed sharp and flat, piano key black.
She came with a group of young painters and sculptors,
men with black hair, dressed in all black.

And there were lots of girls he never knew
or thought he never knew. Memory slows.
Memory goes. Who knows? But women remember.

Z came, in honey-colored dreds again.
When she sat, it was like a light
came from her face. She was the sun,
a Sanskrit song; when lights dimmed,
a star. She sat alone. No one moved in.

Raylene came with her six kids, drove in
from Manhattan, the Little Apple, and asked
to sit in on violin, "fiddle", and did.
She whispered, as she stepped from the stand,
her song done, "I'll always love you.
Now you go sit in," and Calvin did, for all
of those women, he did, and he didn't
do too bad; out of practice, but full of spirit,
like Z, for three songs he, too, lit up the room,
like a blue neon sign in a hot KC night
on the corner of 18th & Vine, he did.

First Sex

Rhonda offers me pot, a roach in her hand. It smokes. I say no.
She says, "Let's smoke this together and then have sex on that
mattress," the mattress on the floor, her bed. I say no. I've never
had sex, don't know. I've never smoked, never had a drink. I'm
19. Rhonda's tall and skinny and older, a grad. student in oboe
performance. Bum reeds line her ceiling; she sticks them up
there, jabs them when they don't work, her knife on the window
sill, the window open. Everyone would hear our cries. "Why
not?" Rhonda says. "Stan and Pam are doing it right now in the
other room." She points to the closed door, her roommate inside.
"They do it quiet-like, like sheep," she says. "Disgusting," she
says. "Make noise! Let it out." Rhonda shows me a photo she
took, a slide of a man with an erection, nude. She must think I'm
gay. I try to kiss her, go home.

II.
like one of Joe's songs

Those quarter note triplets in Mingus's "Goodbye Pork Pie Hat" always get me. There is no sadness like theirs. That sadness, that sadness has lift. It holds the Prez and what he said on sax a few notes longer than anyone needs to. That section of notes going up, then going down, it is what the heart must do, when it beats and hurts, and pumps as it must in cadence over the ostenato of grief and loss; that heart syncopates to rush the blood, to push the pulse, to heal the body that is blue and down and slow. Please let me feel something; let me know you are there and with me. Blood of my body, push me on.

Fables of Faubus

Red-haired, yellow fedora-ed
MP put the LP on and set it
spinning, and the spirit of Mingus
came into the rehearsal room.
We were kids, young men
with guitars and drumsticks
    and saxophones in our hands,
and this was revolution
    we were learning, how
a society tune can turn
    dirty, swift in the middle
of a passage, and strike back,
    quick as a cymbal hit,
at a Southern governor.
Some of us were black,
some of us were white, Latino,
Chicano, Japanese. Some were
from city schools on scholarship,
wearing gold chains, with stitches
along the neckline, knife cuts healed.

I was from the suburbs,
but, as Mapplethorpe said,
they were a good place
to leave. I wanted this music
to flow along my arteries and jitterbug
along the small bones of my arms and legs.

Like One of Joe's Songs

T has me play "Horseshoe Canyon" on brushes,
but before I do, she asks me how I'll play it,
and I say, "It sounds like it has the feel
of one of Joe's tunes," and she says
she was thinking of him when she wrote it.
Joe is gone, dead at 44. He drank himself
into the afterlife, but before he did, he made a go
at the Lawrence scene. I made a list, and he called all
of the places. We brought demo CDs in a briefcase,
and shook hands with managers of coffee shops and bars
and restaurants. Later, when I checked, I found
that all of Joe's CDs were blank. Joe was like that.
T says play it on cajón. I don't want it to sound like Joe.

Megumi

You walked out on a coffee shop gig
because too much of that old piano was flat.
Just laugh. I'll come back. But tonight
I'll apologize, take the empty tip cup and load
drums, go home and dream of better places,
bigger gigs, and players who play *every* gig.

Megumi, where did you go
    with your perfect pitch
    and your voice which could turn
a flat penny on its side, so high—
with your tiny shoes, your short leather skirts
    from Topeka, when we all lived
    in Little Apple Manhattan
and drove in to play big city KC.

Tip Bucket

We're playing on the street, in the square,
    in Barcelona, a little jazz
group with a lot of hand
    drummers—and I'm playing
on trash: milk carton, box,
    Snapple bottle. I brought
sticks, brushes, but no
    drum, packing through.
We have competition: fire
    breathers, belly dancers,
street walkers. One of the fire breathers
    slinks up, kicks over
our tip bucket—plastic, white,
    10 gallon—change and
bills dump, flutter,
    clink into the red brick
street, an eighth note rest, nothing,
    then a flock of hands,
the evening's work gone, quick
    as mottled pigeons, up
from the street and into
    the subterranean night.

Downtown

When the traffic swishes by, while you pace
    the sidewalk, waiting to cross;
when the man in the old green army jacket says,
"That's the path to hell," and you think:
    heaven;
when what you want is tea, and all
    the shop has is coffee;
when the girl you want is slumped
    with a brown paper bag
in an apartment, won't come out, not for you;
when $7 an hour is what you earn, and you
    know the price of every small burger in town,
and you tell yourself you can go without fries;
when at 3 am it's almost just you on this street,
    under this lamp, under these walls, under these awnings,
and you wish you had someone to point out the stars.

Giant Steps

You climb a set of stairs to work, "Giant Steps"
     on your Walkman, and by the time you get to "Naima"
you know what you want more than money, more than time,
     more than love and all of its ways; you want
drums and more drums around you, a bassist in the corner,
a pianist always at his keys, and a man on sax who is full
     of slow fire, who knows
what the subway sounds like, and the traffic jam, and the sidewalk
     shuffle, and the wheels of the bus, how they roll and roll on:

"Ride the dog,"* old man Treadwell says, and each stop
reveals to you places you don't live:
the houses with boards ripped up and holes in all the walls,
the old brick inn, now a crackhouse, and the trailer on the outskirts
of town, its railings splintered and thin;

what you want is not exactly affluence, but a sustained sound,
     like Hammond B3 low whole notes, how they stir the ice
          cubes in your gin—
so very little tonic, how you like it, almost full
of fire, strong enough to let you walk another four songs
 before you show up at your door in Oakland, tap the glass, and
     shuffle in.

*"Ride the Dog": Ride the bus, public transportation

Background Jazz

What I see is the woman seated straight ahead,
as if a line is drawn from
my drum to her body, my eyes
reflected in hers now, for five
quarter note breaths. She looks away
to her husband, spins
the diamond ring on her finger, and
adjusts her bra, adjusts
the pearls at her neck line,
looking now into the eyes
of a much older man
in a camel hair sports coat,
and her husband says, "It was
the initial of my beginning
feelings that there was a
disconnect," and six songs
later, a lady silent auctions
local art, saying, "I'm not
for positive on that."
I turn my eyes to my brushes
that swish over drum head
with the blur a swimming trout makes
just under the water, and I resist
the temptation to whisper ruff them,
or even slap them, or do
a long crescendo roll,
gain that attention, then abruptly stop,
take my small check, and walk
into the night sky silence of stars,
my snare drum in its gray plastic case,
my brushes in a black tuxedo bag,
the strap slung brashly over my shoulder.
Instead, I play on, create that quiet
drone that accompanies company
talk, that allows you to speak
without everyone listening, that allows

you to drink and forget the buzzing
music of your own mind, of your own
simpering problems, while musicians tow
you quietly out to sea.

What Joe Sung on the Porch

What I remember most about our time making music together
was that song "Blue," about how you would play it until I
almost cried missing her. T sat down right beside you, and after
a few minutes of her talk, you said, "Don't sew me a button,"
and turned away, and I knew you knew I couldn't look away.
She was one of those women who made all of her own clothes,
mainly out of patches, and she had taught me how to breathe
and see slow again, but I would not have her. I was married, and
unhappy, and had a son, but I loved all that I was and had, and
nothing truly tempted me away, but my soul orbited her hair,
dreds held by beeswax, and I kept closing my eyes as I played.
And I kept feeling her eyes on my hands on the drum. Her
favorite song was "My Old Friend the Blues," and like a blue
heeler, there it was, our song, Joe singing it, the sun going out all
around us.

Dave Plays the Playboy Mansion

Dave sends me photos over Facebook of the Playboy mansion.
Hugh Hefner is there with a young woman on his arm. He wears
a blood red smoking jacket, sleep jacket, and she wears dark blue
rabbit ears and a matching blue outfit. There's not that much of
it. Dave has on that grin he perfected during our early days, the
dive bar days, the birthday party days, the backyard Fourth of
July days, the wedding gig days. Dave's made it, and he sent me
pictures, and I wonder where it might have gone had I stayed and
played drums for him for ten or 15 years, put the books away and
put my heart across the drums, played them with that vigor I had
at 20, at 21. I'm not old. I still drum. I play in four local groups,
and I play out at least once a month. But I don't drum for money.
Not really. And do I miss it? Only when I'm behind my drums,
in the darkness of the coffee shop, when I look up, and a few
ones go into the jar, when I notice that I could play this way all
night without thinking—my hands know just what to do—when
I realize I could have been playing jazz, in a big band, behind
Dave, at somewhere like the Playboy Mansion, and afterwards
some young woman could come calling me by name. I don't
miss it that much. It only comes back when I play.

After Anna's First Drum Circle

I've been talking to my ancestors today
    through this drum, the way
we've spoken for centuries—with hands,
    with breath. Drums and fire,
what kept the jaguars away.

Dee

One of my former students is living in a tent by the river.
It's the dark, first real night of winter
in Kansas, where there are no mountains to stop
the chill wind. "More time to write," she says.
"No assignments. No job. No one to answer to ever,"
a type writer hung from her hiking pack,
a sheaf of single-space papers in her waterproof bag.
"That way, nothing will happen to them," she says.
"Nothing." I worry for her in this time of cold,
in the woods, Winter with her, a man with treebark
black dreds, a white guy, her age. I write her a letter,
send it to the Lawrence shelter, send her
the school literary magazine, her poem
on page six: what we take with us, what
we carry. I think I'll send her some cash.

* I was in town playing our regular, acoustic, original folk and blues gig
at Aimee's Coffee (1025 Mass). I was living in Emporia, 83 miles from
Lawrence. Dee came, wanted me to look at her poems. When our "poetry
moment" came during the gig, 10 minutes of poetry as an intermission to the
music, and I had the mic, I asked Dee to sit in with me, to read. She did. The
room seemed to brighten to her. And, though she blushed at first and covered
her face, when she took the mic, she read with wisdom and passion and fury,
about towns that leave their artists to the woods.

Lisa Calls from Boulder Colorado
for Lisa

Lisa calls from her motel. She has locked
herself out. She's in the cold, keyless, somewhere
    in lonesome Boulder.

Her guitar inside, she can't sing and strum
while she waits. She walked down, knocked, asked the manager
    to help her in, at a small Colorado stop; she waits,

just off the highway, a folk gathering just two miles
down the road. She waits outside on the motel walk,
    the others in tents, hunkered into a chill Colorado night,

campfires low and smoking, the stars
out and bright like cherry cig tips held by Colorado gods

that ash snow in early winter. But even in summer
    it can be cold, August,
and my lover is locked out, calling, asking what to do
    about cold quiet Colorado.

Forget every bird
that dares sing during this season
when we hunker together under
bare black limbs.
Your voice is the one I tune to
when the streets grow cold
and empty—and when
the traffic becomes too much.
I wipe the salt
from my truck's frame.
I crack the window, listen
for your voice among the steel alders
and glass clouds.

for Lisa

III.
what about love?

Liz Catches Stars

Elizabeth could catch shooting stars
    on her tongue.
We used to catch snowflakes together.
Then she went bigger—and for fire.
Nights, I saw her up on Suicide Hill
    by 51st Street Coffee House
at the edge of where campus
    turns back into city—
and Liz was *all* city,
hot stars on her tongue,
the night raining fire
    into her red mane of hair,
and she took those small comets
    of rock and of fire,
like rain or like snowflakes
    onto her tongue.

Map of My Heart

Ask me to map my heart
    in '94, and I could show you
who I was and who I loved, brave model/photographer
Amber, with her hands on the metal negative spools,
she agitates in the dark; the photo chemicals
swish with her touch, and she leans into me in red light,
and her kiss is like a gold rimmed glass, champagne,
sweet and sudden, when a party takes to the rain,
to blacktop, to the city streets, and Amber and I watch
from her new apartment window, through her blue tulle
curtains: the Sheraton, Sheraton, red letters
along the top of night; we watch the couplings come
through yellow windows and pray to the altar
of one night stands, our hands together, our bodies naked,
all of Amber's lights off, a candle lit in the center of her room.

At 21

"Guess she gave you things
I couldn't give to you."
("Someone Like You" *Adele 21*)

The tantric goddess,
with her many hands,
something new in each grip—

a crown, a tiny horse, a sword,
some grapes.

"Take it, if you want it,"
Maryanna says, the large popcorn tub
in her lap, our only movie date.

Gwen

Gwen quit coming to class,
but before she did, she talked about how
she needed money and had started modeling
for the art dept. She invited me to come.
I don't draw much anymore, but after Gwen
was gone for a week and a half, I went,
and I wrote while she modeled.
The guy beside me, in his 50s, drew
a beautiful portrait of Gwen's
young, nude figure, with the body
of a dragon underneath.
I put $30 in the coffee can,
hoping it might help
bring Gwen back to class.
After the session, Gwen came out
in a purple robe and talked to me
outside by the arched stone doorway
in the darkness. She offered me
a cigarette, and I tried to smoke,
and we talked, the smoke,
like spirits, around us, calling.

Monday morning, Gwen was back
in class, that red coffee can on her desk,
the lid pushed on tight, her eyes
like wet blue water color paint.

In Gwen's First Letter

In her letter, she says
    she likes skinny dipping
at night in the lake
    out behind her parents' house
where she is living, with her two toddler daughters,
    in the basement. She says
I should come visit. She read what I wrote
    in her journals, sat near the front of the class,
contacts me now, seven years later. Yes, I remember
    you. Yes, you have lots of talent, I think.
No, I don't have any of your poems and papers
    tucked away in my glove box or in a big oak chest.

White Tea

I would have kissed you
    after you made me white tea
with lemon and honey and put the saucer
    into my hand and brushed by me,
your breasts against my back,
    on the way to the tea towel,
but your husband called down
    from his bedroom, where he was suffering
from West Nile, and your voice changed
    as you answered him, and it was as if
he entered the room. A beat, and we all changed
    back. You're his. I'm just a guest. Love flies
on orange butterfly wings, and the mind digs in,
    cranks the tarnished wheel of the music box that sticks,
and I sip my tea and imagine I am tasting your warm lips.

Spices

I pour the *Mrs. Dash* into my cupped palm,
then scrape my hands together, let the spices
fall onto the tops of the burgers.
My ex-wife taught me this, press
every spice, scrape the goodness out.

With her, the red sauce was the thing;
she'd simmer that marinara for hours,
like prepping for a kiss or an argument:
heat, wait, stir.

Your Almost Blunted Purpose

Sound of milk steamer
and coffee grinder. Careless slap
of wet flip flops
over hardwood floor: what it is
to be in the posh downtown Starbuck's
in April. But you must stop looking
at their shiny hair and shiny
legs and sports-bra-lofted breasts and toes
painted so very very red, and write.
You are not the only one
in Starbuck's. You have things to do,
and they are here to meet someone else—
or want only to be seen
by some much much younger men,
men in skinny jeans, with new
bronze watches on their wrists.

Samantha's twin toddler sons
crawled down the flight of wooden stairs
backwards one step at a time. They scooted
their way, and I crouched and went with them.
Samantha came last. She had seen this
before. It was a marvel, how fast they went,
unafraid, butt-first, not stopping
until they touched the tile floor by the front door.
We went out and onto the snow-packed sidewalk
and across the street and into the city park.
I could see tears in Samantha's eyes,
which she said were from the November wind,
which was blowing her green scarf around
her red hair, but perhaps I had caused it,
some grief, a lonely married man escorting
toddlers and a single mother into the city park.

Samantha's husband had gone crazy and left her
for a VJ he found on the web.
I too had once gone crazy,
but I swore I would not go crazy again.

A Body of Love

In the Hays House, we wait half an hour
for buttermilk-battered, skillet-fried chicken,
and I take it between my teeth, wanting
to get every last browned niblet
of what was once chicken skin
between my lips, balanced on my tongue,
crushed between my teeth with
careless chops. I have given in
to my impulses, to my taste, to my stomach,
and to those senses I do not use enough—
all beyond the eyes, moving
to the stomach and the tongue
letting my teeth take over
and my lips, giving in to the range
and radar of my nose.

As for touch, if it feels good to the skin, take it in-
to your hand, press it against a cheek,
hold it on the inside of your arm or wrist
until you have its warmth, its texture
in memory. Let it sink into your skin,
past skin, into muscle until it communes
with bone, sinks into marrow.
Does the body remember better than the brain?

When my body remembers you
through my eyes that tracked and held
as you ran-can-canned in, hipped in—
as you moved in as a petal wind
in through the tunnels of my nostrils,
down the drop of the throat, and climbed
and sped along the lines of my forehead and brow,
as you swiveled and swayed, a night-skirt spirit
in the hairs on my arms, you were
in all the blood that sped to my face
and to the front of my head, in every

quick full breath, in every finger flexing,
in every part of my body charging and readying,
growing hot and strong and supple for your full love—
my body now a body of love.

for Lisa

The Husband's Complaint

Bea and I had sex
in empty campus chapels late at night,
alongside pianos and drums in campus practice rooms,
in sleeping bags, after class in rooms packed
with desks, and even once in a giant clawfoot tub
built for three. It was as if our loins were wounds
that could only be salved by sex.

I thought grad. school would lead my wife and I
to tons of passionate sex.
Instead, it led to separate beds.

City Cartography with Lisa

I walked up three flights of blue stairs
    to your apartment every weekend, a line
as in the Peanuts, dotted and circuitous,
made my way from suburb to city
to see you, knocked on your thick wooden door
and waited. You would be in your robe and ask me
to sit at your kitchen table, where I would watch
the plaza holiday lights play yellows and reds
on your walls and watch headlights draw white cones
in black, rainy streets; umbrellas popped up;
and we would walk to the book store, get coffee,
see the city move like a giant towards morning,
and we were almost underfoot.

VI.
travel & place

East off Highway 77, Dusk

Heather light, evening light,
    lemon rind light, hand hold light,
quail hovel light, goldentime light,
    first kiss, fishing hole light;
this is when the starlings fly
    into shelter belts; the hawks
find a branch, land, wait
for prairie mice to come from holes
and cast swift shadows
    in the tight grass, for wings
to flourish and lift; one dive
and it's done; we all eat this light up,
bask like children on lawns in last light,
the light at the end of the earth;
sun sinks, earth crests, and the sun's done.
Twilight and its small stars come.

*Ekphrasis on Dave Leiker's digital color photo (2005): "Flint Hills Side Road, Under a Clearing Sky after a Storm, East off Highway 77 – Morris County, Kansas"

Wild Horses & Road

Wild horses lie down on blacktop
for some warmth in the pass
in the middle of winter, horses stretched out
on road, and sometimes a car comes
and hits one, breaking body, breaking legs,
and Sam has to come with the gun
my father gave him, the long rifle, and end it,
put a bullet in the head, send
the horse home: skies above, valleys below,
and mountains, mountains all around.

Sam: a wilderness ranger based in Caliente, Nevada; my sister's husband
long rifle: 270 Remington bolt action

Pictographs Somewhere in the Pahrocs

Sam said the archeologist had an old old record
of Piute pictographs in the area miles east
of Ash Springs Rock Art Site and dared Sam
        to find the spot.
We visit, and Sam takes me to the shaded crevice,
a hole beneath a big rock, and I climb in,
and in the blue-purple light
I find bright orange men with long arms,
a sun with rays like aster petals,
and water, the wavy lines, the spirit paths.
Bright as an orange crayon, vivid as if painted
just yesterday, here they are, the marks
a shaman made some thousand years ago, paintings
huddled in the half dark, or just sleeping, as snakes
do, hidden from the high white Mohave sun,
waiting for someone, like us, to come look.

Steamboat Erupts

I.
Sam was in his tent in the backcountry
when it happened, the earth opening
and sending water up and out, water
spouting from Steamboat Geyser,
one that had not erupted in hundreds of years,
but who could know this? Steamboat erupts,
fiercer than Old Faithful, and more glorious.
Sam said, "It felt like the end of the world."

II.
A group of young people in dreadlocks stopped
their walk across the hot pools, stood in the middle
of the water, listening; something was happening; something
was quaking and bringing bubbles up,
and Doug, the park photographer, moved quick
that morning, his equipment pulsing, the indicator eyes
blinking green and red, as he drove, then ran; and the park
    biologists,
they moved slowly in the beat-up brown park pickup truck
toward where they knew the water would be.

III.
First, the steam: a cloud caught,
tethered to ground, stuck. Then, water:
a gush of water up and up, firehose
of hot hot water shot up, everything
above it a white and grey cloud; mist and hot rain, fire rain.
The buffalo come from their long green walk and wait,
and lift their heads in the second round of water,
luke warm water, dull root, deep underground pool,
now like rain.

When Street Lamps Click on

Sun's down, and the lamp posts click on,
not all at once, but in an enigmatic order,
like when electrons jump valence circles
or when one brilliant idea comes at once
to three people in distant continents.
It comes like monks come into enlightenment;
their foreheads seem to glow, and each blossoms,
a separate pale cherry tree flower, each
on a different limb of the tree, bright
like when Christmas lights come on
on a sapling planted in a city sidewalk—
all of those lights, faint and teary-eyed, twinkle,
distant and mysterious as the stars.

Skate Party

J skates oblong laps around the rink. He wobbles.
J's 15, with thick oval glasses, fish bowls,
and white iPod cords always run from his ears.
I wonder about J, who comes over about once a month
and asks me to tune his acoustic guitar,
which I can do, because my wife plays, and has a tuner,
but his pegs swivel and are reluctant to catch.
His is a garage sale guitar, and I have heard him strumming it
arrhythmically out back. Lisa said, "What's that?"
And I said, "J on guitar. He's learning." He'll learn.
We'll all learn, like the elk on their first steps,
rising from birth. They don't leap up and fly,
but, on broomstick legs, they do move.
They totter, and after a spell, they lean into air,
head first, push toward the center
of the clearing, drive toward the middle
of the now standing, now moving, herd.

Winter and its freeze
gathers the ground and traps the windows
in its fingers, webs, branches of frost,
Lichtenberg figures. Cold, like lightning,
hits and knicks and blooms. Death
is only cold. We grow cold and stop,
cease. Pray the spirit gets out
before the ice sets in.

Birds Here

The guys in the back of the Suburban
would down that last swig of Coors,
crinkle the cans, and barrel out
of the truck, the tops of their shot guns
pointed up and out. "Birds here"
someone would shout, and the youngest
of the men would run quick across the dirt road
and jump the ditch and jump the barbed wire fence,
and shots would go off, birds fall, and the men
would run and catch what they had got,
swinging the birds, ringing the necks
and pulling the heads off, as they stomped back to the truck.

Pheasant Hunting Sketch

Alvin swings the bird
    by the neck.
He stomps the head
    and yanks it off.
Blood specks fall
    onto the tall prairie grass
and onto his jeans. Alvin tosses
    the rest into the truck,
and that city lawyer
    we've brought along
bends and retches
    into new snow.

At the Curtis Café

in Stafford, Kansas

When I die, I will rise in a small town diner
with a seat that faces the Main Street window,
and all of the silverware and waterglasses and tabletops
will shine with afternoon light, and I will know no one
who comes in through the front door and sits and eats.
We will all watch the street lamps illuminate
the uneven brick street and wait
for afternoon to pass on into evening, full of shadows
jagged and irregular, the street filling up
with darkness in the way coffee fills up a pale coffee cup.

ABOUT THE AUTHOR:

Kevin Rabas co-directs the creative writing program at Emporia State and edits *Flint Hills Review*. His books include: *Bird's Horn*, *Lisa's Flying Electric Piano*, a Kansas Notable Book and Nelson Poetry Book Award winner, and *Spider Face: stories*. Rabas is the winner of the Langston Hughes Award for Poetry, the Victor Contoski Poetry Award, the Jerome Johanning Playwriting Award, and the Salina New Voice Award.

PRIMARY CURRENT INFLUENCES:
Literary: Kim Addonizio (*Tell Me*), Thomas Lux, Tim Seibles, Jonathan Holden, N. Shange, Sam Shepard, David Auburn (*Proof*), Dorianne Laux, Wendell Berry, William Stafford, Langston Hughes, Yusef Komunyakaa, Michael Ondaatje, Michael Ardnt (*Little Miss Sunshine*), Alan Ball (*American Beauty*), Woody Allen (*Hannah & Her Sisters*), Nora Ephron (*When Harry Met Sally…*), Rachel Cohn and David Levithan (*Nick & Norah's Infinite Play-List*).

Musical: Sonny Kenner, Keith Jarrett (*The Koln Concert, Tribute*: "U Dance"), John Coltrane (*Coltrane's Sound*: "Equinox"), Claude "Fiddler" Williams (*King of Kansas City*), Mark Lowrey (*Live at Jardine's*), Leonard Cohen, Josh Ritter, Patty Griffin (*1000 Kisses*), Adele (*21*).

ABOUT THE PAINTER:

Jennifer Rivera is an abstract expressionist painter who works primarily with acrylics on canvas. Known for edgy and emotionally evocative abstract paintings which are often inspired by poetry, she employs the use of texture, bold strokes, and rich colors in her work. Her artwork has appeared in numerous magazines and she was named one of Kansas City's top five visual artists in *KC Magazine* in 2010 and 2011. Rivera's work is collected by both private and corporate clients from across the country, and has been exhibited in galleries and museums.

From Rivera's artist's statement:
"I have always been fascinated with the rhythm of words in various forms. I create from an emotional place rather than a visual one and phrases, lyrics, and poetry offer an abundance of inspiration for me. I enjoy the challenge of abstracting these words and recreating them into another art form."

Rivera's website is www.artistjenniferrivera.com

Sonny Kenner on the Sonnyside of the Street

The popular standard "On the Sunny Side of the Street" could have been written for guitarist Sonny Kenner. He liked the "On the Sunny Side" so much that he adopted it as his theme song, performing it as "Sonnyside of the Street." An optimist with a big smile and twinkling gray eyes, Sonny brightened the lives of those he met and entertained during his long musical career.

Sonny came of age musically in Kansas City's 18th and Vine district, playing alongside Jay McShann, Charlie Parker, and other jazz legends. At age five he constructed a guitar from a cigar box and rubber band. Four years later, his mother bought him a Harmony guitar. While attending high school, he formed his first group, the Five Aces with pianist Larry Cummings. After a stint with the legendary Red Hot Scamps, Sonny toured nationally and recorded with Sonny Thompson, a popular pianist known as the "cat on the keys."

In 1955, Sonny was drafted into the Army. While stationed in Germany, he joined the Armed Services 8th Division Band. At the request of his commanding officer, he formed the European Jazz Quartet with other service members. The quartet toured bases across Germany. During his off time, Sonny played Viennese waltzes and polkas for the locals.

Once discharged in 1959, Sonny settled down in Los Angeles where he became an in-demand sideman and session musician. He played and recorded with a wide variety of groups and artists including the Crusaders, James Brown, Little Richard, and Jimmy Witherspoon. His impassioned guitar solo powered the Rivington's novelty hit "Papa-Oom-Mow-Mow."

In 1965, Sonny moved back to Kansas City, where he and his wife Sarah raised five children. For the rest of his life, Sonny maintained his base in Kansas City. He taught music lessons at the Charlie Parker Memorial Foundation and played clubs and festivals with his own group. He was noted for his broad musical repertoire that embraced soul, R & B, blues, jazz, classical, pop, country western, rock, and later hip hop and reggae. When Sonny was onstage, no request from the audience was left unfilled. Night after night, he packed the dance floor at the Levee and other clubs in Kansas City, directing the dancers' feet to "The Sonnyside of the Street."

—Chuck Haddix, jazz historian and director, MARR Sound Archive, UMKC; coauthor of *Kansas City Jazz: From Ragtime to Bebop— A History* (Oxford Press)

www.ingramcontent.com/pod-product-compliance
Lightning Source LLC
Chambersburg PA
CBHW062027040426
42447CB00010B/2170